Richard Kell was born in Co. Cork in 1927 and was educated mainly in Belfast and Dublin. He lives in Newcastle-upon-Tyne at whose Polytechnic—now the University of Northumbria—he taught literature for many years. He is a widower, and the father of two sons (the elder deceased in 1995) and two daughters. His *Collected Poems 1962-1993* was published recently by Lagan Press. *The Banyan Book*, a reflective journal of 650,000 words, is now in typescript, and he is working on its shorter successor, *The Rowan Book*. He is a co-editor of the magazine *Other Poetry*.

By the same author

Poetry
Control Tower
Differences
The Broken Circle
Humours
In Praise of Warmth:
New & Selected Poems
Rock and Water
Collected Poems 1962-1993

UNDER THE RAINBOW

UNDER THE RAINBOW

RICHARD KELL

LAGAN PRESS
BELFAST
2003

Acknowledgements
The publishers and author would like to thank the editors of the following publications, where a number of the poems in this collection first appeared: *Books Ireland, Céide, Cyphers, Five Irish Poets* (anthology), *Galway Advertiser, Honest Ulsterman, Iota, Orbis, Poetry Ireland Review, Poetry Review* and *Stand Magazine*.

Published by
Lagan Press
138 University Avenue
Belfast BT7 1GZ

© Richard Kell

The moral right of the author has been asserted.

ISBN: 1 873687 88 5
Author: Kell, Richard
Title: Under the Rainbow
2003

Set in Palatino
Printed by Noel Murphy Printing, Belfast

for Enid Radcliffe

THE NAMING

Elephant, flea
and chimpanzee,
clingfish, ray,
condor and jay,
each one heard
a clarion word
as human sight,
soul's delight,
newly received
all that lived.
Now Eve drifts
on tiny shifts
of art, a wife
with real life!

In this cross-acrostic, the letters running diagonally from top left to bottom right spell the name of the dedicatee. The title refers also to Blake's 'Adam Naming the Beasts' and 'Eve Naming the Birds'—RK

CONTENTS

I

Digswell Water (1955)	15
Son and Father	17
The Souvenirs	19
Lights	20
Silver	21
The Last Visit	23
Reservoir	25
Ada	26
Our Place	29
How Things Have Changed	30
The Life of Brian	31
The Ashtray	32
Energies	33
After a Phonecall	34
The Little Scorpions	35
A Winged Visitor	36
Achill	38
The Waters of Achill	40
Kindly December	41
Border Crossings	43
On the Wind	44
Visiting Keem	46
The Settlement	48
In the Bus Shelter	51
The Circling Beam	52
Epithalamion (1992)	53
Attractions	54
To Jon Silkin (1930-1997)	55
The Language Man	56
Poetry Gigs, 1994	57
Biographies (1959)	58
The Song of the Crossword Puzzler (1990)	59

II

To William Carlos Williams	63
From a Parson's Journal	64
Aztec Picture	65
After the Briefing	66
Electricity	67
The Ways of Providence	68
Songs of Praise	69
What Comes Naturally	70
The Idealist	71
Under the Rainbow	72
Evolution	73
Laziness	75
Femina: A Rhapsody	77
Nocturne	78
At the Moonlit Pool: A Pastoral	79
The Utopian	80
Theologies	81
A Professor to Some Friends	82
First Person	86
For the Millennium Prayerbook	87
Recycling	88
Keeping Up	89
Heisenberg in Copenhagen	90
The Seeker	91
To the Lady of Norwich	95

PART ONE

DIGSWELL WATER (1955)
for Muriel

So we had to trespass to be ourselves,
startle somebody's fish where I could sit
with nothing on in a bowl of coloured gravel
under the weir, up to my neck in bubbles,
and you with the baby kicking beneath your bright
and confident smock might paddle and envy me.

Well, it was worth being caught by the river keeper
to find again that we were born loafers
and innocent as the lark with his little bells
or the child in the warm cradle of your body.
When drowsy churches rang for sin's recital,
being so blest a pagan I recalled
not even the world's deep wounds. For you were lovely
there in the shining grass, and I content
with my head across your thighs and the opulent sun
showering its largest through the evening air.

Correct me, death, if I am too complacent—
yet I shall only shrug at you, knowing well
complacency's a luxury that's rare
for one whose peace of mind is volatile.
Tomorrow I shall be half the self I am
and half the one that's made to cope with schemes
of measured give and take, to earn a living,
provide a home of sorts; but made with care
out of materials that are my own
however faulty, granting no concession
unsigned by courage, honesty, and love.
Such at least is the credo—plain, concise
and resonant: its trial is resumed
with cheerful irony on Monday mornings.

Meanwhile I think of you, dear wife, dear friend,
of your smiling green eyes and your brilliant smock

and the precious burden that you bear so sweetly;
of plunging my head into the purring water
and lying lazy under the sabbath sun,
glad of occasional joy and grateful always
for being in first love with you once in a while.

SON AND FATHER
i.m. Colin Kell, 1955-1995

You were the wild one. Early accident-prone,
you tumbled down the stairs; in boyhood crashed—
backwards, thank heaven—through a bay window;
later, rebel away from home, got done
for speeding, loafed, explored the world of drugs.

Knowing you weren't the type to settle down,
you took a ranging job—drove sonorous
artics as far as Russia, then along
the highways of the States. My letters, rare
as yours, sent love and slightly envious praise.

We all want something more that's also different:
one self keeps doing its duty while another
rattles the exit doors to lives unlived.
I saw myself roving across Nevada;
you thought you'd like to study, even write—

even, you told me years ago, to be
a playboy with a yacht. But the handsome smile
and athletic build weren't everything: you worked
and worried, cared as husband and stepfather,
left many in deep sorrow when you died.

Resented government, loathed the abuse of power.
I have two letters—one above your name
from a local paper, the other a union's praise
for your commitment. Over a northern pint
you said, smiling in hope, 'an anarchist'.

But nothing was quite as moving as the words
of our friendly neighbours' son, recalling how,
when you were in your teens and he a child,
you championed him against the local bully.
Justice, compassion—the best of politics.

Your mother died by drowning at fifty-two,
you by a kind of drowning in your prime.
Why? Conjectures prowl in the infra-red,
some frightening. Maybe justice and compassion
are only human, only in beings like you.

THE SOUVENIRS
i.m. Colin Kell, 1955-1995

I recall with love
that pointed summit carved
on blue in the warm light,
you strongly climbing
while I paused for breath;
a wasp and a wood pigeon
beside the cairn, where someone's
orange peel and pips
were drying on a flat stone,
and the hazed calm of Loch Etive
deep in a bed of hills.

Back home, I scraped and washed
the rough wayside sticks we'd used,
with clear varnish turned
their bony timber into gold,
and propped them in the room
where they are still gleaming.
Since then, mine has felt
sunlight and earth; yours
—taller, richly brindled—
only the walled air, and once
an old hand bringing news.

LIGHTS
for Peter, Sue, and Molly (1995)—with gratitude

In flaky clouds, the white
shine of a full moon,

far out on the moor's dark sea
a prickle of yellow lamps,

and close to hand the torch
my dear host provided:

so little, such a lot
to help me with the night.

SILVER
for Enid and other dear ones

When I was back, alone in this memoried house,
you told me over the phone
how glad you were your grandfather clock was home
after several decades. 'That makes two,' I thought,
'the grandfather clock and you.' I wish
both you and him the happiness both deserve
after all those years in the South—
you as wife and mother and part professional, still
going on with a kindly will though deeply hurt.
At the end of the long journey, handyman Rob
performed such a magical job, you said, that now
the pendulum swings unfailingly; never mind
that the old tick-tocking heart
can't quite keep time with Greenwich.
'Does he still chime?' I asked. You told me he did—
'a lovely silvery chime'. Five minutes later
I heard him over the phone. I'm going to love
that musical voice again when I'm not alone,
when sometimes I am sharing with you and him
your new-found place in the North.

During an afternoon as dad and granddad
I'd heard the silvery laughter
of little Rachel and Sam. A cautious hand
had sampled the texture of my silvery beard!
Later, when we were walking up to the woods
beside a silvery stream, I said
that surely the sound of tumbling water is one of the
loveliest sounds in the world. Hearing it now
in my mind, I think of gamelan tones as well,
and clinking cowbells, and then of the tiny bell—
with a lighter, clearer voice—I hung in a pram
some forty years ago, after
I'd had it dipped in silver. Memory tolls
for a man who died too young—

son, brother, uncle, no longer here
to share the friendly words and the friendly laughter.

   Thanks for ringing me when I came back home
to a house no longer home. It was good to hear
the voice I love, and a new one joining in.
I said to myself 'Three hearts are beating still,
all grand ones!' Far too bright
for sentimentality, you apologised
for a sentimental thought; forgive me mine.
But I think in our veteran years we have a right
to symbolism at least. What better then
than an old clock striking ten?
Fast or slow, no matter: it's only doing
what humans asked, imposing on life's flow
an arithmetic they needed, so why complain
when the task's no longer urgent? Aren't we free
to call the bluff of time? The peaceful clock
says 'Oh you are, you are. Just live like me.
Though I tick and tock, my silvery chime is meant
simply as music. Listen, and learn to *be*.'

THE LAST VISIT
i.m. Irene Kell, née Musgrave, 1900-1997

Mother, you were almost
someone I'd never known—your face
a tawny wood carving,
no longer of any time or region;
eyes clouded, body-flesh
thin and slack on warped bones.

And oh your voice, your voice—
wordless, piping only
in the release of shallow breaths.
But the old will was there in your trying hard
to speak, and when we held hands
the way you gripped my thumb,
as I must have gripped yours nearly
seventy years ago.

Did you know me? I like to think
you did but couldn't say,
and saw me too although your eyes
were grey pools without lustre,
the pupils faded out.

I had to believe we were taking turns, that I
made memories glow—how strange,
two or three times, those cries
I hoped were happy laughter—and that you
were replying. 'Yes,' I said,
'I'm listening ... yes ... yes'—
gently desperate, wondering if you needed
'no' sometimes (or more), if *you* were wondering...

The old will showed again in the way
you tensed your body, urged it
forward from the pillows as your voice
groped in parts that wouldn't work. I said

'You're finding it hard to shape words,
but I'm listening all the same.'

   How many breaths in ninety-seven years?
How many times of eating, talking—
efforts of lips, teeth, tongue? Our weird communion
paused when a nurse brought in the pap. I watched
your mouth sucking the savoury from a spoon,
then said 'May I take over?'

   Apple and custard. You seemed to understand
that this was more than feeding and being fed—
opened your mouth wide for every spoonful
(did I need coaxing seventy years ago?),
as though to say 'You know what I'm trying to say'.

   I looked in your clouded eyes,
wondering again if you could see me,
kissed your forehead, said
'Goodbye—we all love you', and walked away.
Oh mother, mother, may heaven grant we shared
something deeper in those two hours
than we had done with words in twenty years.

RESERVOIR

No one bathes here. A child
could take one step from shallows into
black fathoms, drop
through roof or branches or on rusting
barbs. 'They created
a monster,' the nephew says.

From the feet of his little girl
to shadowy hills, the lake spreads
miles of silver. She picks stones,
with lusty swing
plops them into ripples.
Idyllic, the uncle thinks.

He gives her carefully chosen whites,
receives lumpy browns
that tell him he's accepted,
lobs them in. Finds rare
skimmers with his nephew
and flips them across the sleek water.

ADA
in memory long after

Great-aunt, 'Auntie' to us, let me tell you now
how much I loved and love you, and how little
I know of your spinsterhood. Did you take a vow
in secret (heart-warmed Wesleyan) to forego
marriage for saintly reasons? Did you settle
for singleness because you thought you were plain,
comparing yourself with sisters?—or were you vain
and hard to please? Never! Did some young man
promise then let you down?

Questions, questions... Ada, why did we all—
generations after the hallelujahs,
the testimonies, the tears—
keep quiet about what matters?
Officially what mattered was Christ and soul
and work—fine for those who were up to it,
but how about those for whom the patient role
was wrong, whose deepest feelings could never fit
their family-album smile?

One thing you did reveal was how you cared
in earlier years for Purdon till he died.
You were so gentle, so naturally loving
with us as well, but maybe a little sad,
that I've often wondered if the Holy Word
was enough, or if you grieved not to have had
some children of your own.
Anyway there you were, the only sister
unmarried and alone.

Grandpa Musgrave managed the big hotel;
you were the manageress, your final home
a top-floor room with a view—
the sweet factory, Patrick's Bridge, a gleam
of the River Lee. I still remember well

those fumes of mint and caramel; how we saw,
as visitors once, a thick soft ribbon glide
towards its destiny in the Blissful Jaw!
Musgrave Brothers meant profit, chapel, God—

securely, in any order. There was coal
as well as toffee; a laundry, a wholesale firm.
The magnificent Metropole
was 'The Finest [the One?] Unlicensed Hotel in Ireland';
and we—Donald and I
on holiday from Belfast—were little princes,
made welcome in the office, the Glory Hole,
the kitchen; best of all Room Ninety-Six,
above it only the roof-walk and the sky.

Dear Ada, how I loved the factory smell
and the jam-and-banana sandwiches! But now,
ageing as you were then,
I bless your readings mainly—so well intended,
so simply mixed, like *Captain January*
along with *The Pilgrim's Progress*. Heaven-and-Hell
in a classic was good for me
as well as thrilling, but brought me in the end
(thank you, and please forgive!) to the skies of Zen.

With you we gathered blackberries, had picnics
in green corners where wasps arrived to sample
our juicy treats. You took me to the Savoy
for celebrity concerts, films; were disappointed
if I chose Myrna Loy
or Cagney or Wayne when you picked Shirley Temple.
Kreisler was great. Tauber we had to miss;
but we heard him warming up in the 'royal' suite,
received a monocled smile and a wafted kiss.

Later, some illness. You were shrunk and pale,
propped on pillows, wearing a blue-green cardie.
I remember the sunny window, you in tears.

Loving Granny as well,
and God of course, and knowing how He and we
all loved each other, how could I understand
why she reproached you? After so many years
perhaps I do. Caring is partly hell,
a rock's endurance as it wears to sand.

But that's in time: there are also grains of love,
some of them gold, held fast in memories, poems,
snaps in the family album. Seeing you grieve,
we felt for you—small 'nephew' and big sister.
I think you wept knowing there was no reprieve,
no place for you between
the lonely nursing home and the silent grave.
How could she help, or I? We hugged and kissed you,
said goodbye, returned to the April shine.

OUR PLACE

Ageing, it will become
a huge red globe, a swelling hell
for Mercury, Venus, Earth;
later a heart, its pulse millennia-slow;
finally a flood of luminous blue-red gas
to the farthest planets, and a contracted core.
White dwarf will cinder then to black—
so heavy a death
that a granule would weigh tons.

Meanwhile, on days like this,
it glows kindly. Blossoms flame,
a football thuds on the grass
and a terrier's joining in.
I trudge through the park with my helpful stick
to catch the post, while someone who's even older
drives his invalid buggy along the path,
his shopping stowed in the rack.
When he smiles and says good morning, I do the same.

HOW THINGS HAVE CHANGED

It comes to me now from larger tits.
I brave a pert spring morning
to lift the day's supply,
and find around one milkwhite neck
a triumphant paper collar.
Have you won, it crows,
a mountain bike?
Get up 'n' go, it hectors (mocking
my journey to the doorstep),
then *Look under semi-skimmed bottle tops—*
Win mountain bikes
Win rollerblades
Win skateboards
Win clock radios—
Ask your milkman.
And where, I wonder,
did this exuberance begin?
Waterford, says the collar.
Not all that far from where,
sixty-nine years ago,
I guzzled my first food.

THE LIFE OF BRIAN

Brian, employed in Saudi Arabia, favours
rigorous laws and the chopping off of hands,
but finds it a rewarding sideline
to sell illegal liquor.
Recounting which, I add with smug humility,
lifting a packet of Marlboro, 'Of course
I can't throw stones: relying on these
is just as bad in a way.'
'Worse,' a friend obliges, and explains
with quiet authority that the land
cultivated by the tobacco barons
could have been used to feed the poor.
Right—and though he doesn't say so,
who but a hypocrite
would nod to his opinions while diffusing
a shifty veil of smoke?
Brian, frankly contemptuous of caring
for any but number one—
doing quite nicely money-wise,
enjoying far from his wife
a supply of emancipated nurses,
and keen, for his future security,
on the restoration of hanging
in the United Kingdom—puts me to shame:
personal enterprise is more appealing
than indolent goodwill.
I'll shove my store of twenties
firmly into the dustbin, doing my bit
for the Third World, and rising
a notch or two in my friend's judgement.
Yes, quite soon, when I'm feeling up to it.

THE ASHTRAY

Stubbing my cigarette
while thinking
of something else
I found it
making firm rings
from the centre outwards
clearing away the ash
the butts
the dead matches
till there appeared
shining coldly
a perfect glass sun

ENERGIES
for Enid Radcliffe

Finite and unbounded,
the limpid globe you gave me
stands on my windowsill,
and on sunny days
the whirligig inside
is a faintly tinkling
flicker of black and white,
its tiny sails sharing
with us in their own way
a breeze of light.

AFTER A PHONECALL
for Enid Radcliffe

Thank you for telling me your dream.
If only I could dream it too—
I mean, could make myself become
the happy me being dreamed by you!

Given that there's no earthly way
of sharing someone else's head,
it warmed my heart to hear you say
I felt so real in your bed.

What warms me now is 'As above,
below'. Though Plato may appear
less than platonic, how I'll love
being more than dreamed-of when you're here!

THE LITTLE SCORPIONS

The little scorpions of the dockyard wall
sleep in their crevices almost through the year,
wake now and then to grab a passing meal
or copulate, and fall asleep once more.

A WINGED VISITOR

To me, no entomologist,
what crawled on the window's Eiger
looked like a male ant.
Whether he saw himself as guest,
prisoner, pioneer, or beggar,
was quite beyond me; but since he spent
all afternoon on the precipice
the second seemed most likely.
I thought 'They must be driven mad
when transparency makes a promise
it doesn't keep—when all that light
stays torturingly solid.'

Mostly I've had wasps and bees.
It was simple to put their plastic cup
(transparent also) round a body
that didn't bounce and skitter, then to ease
the cardboard in until the trap
closed. If he was bothered
he gave no sign at all:
just crept—enquiringly, it seemed—
around the humble dome and floor
of his temporary cell,
a moment away from being redeemed,
launched into real wing-delighting air.

Offered the whole sky
he still clung to his tiny board,
then suddenly got the message
and flitted like an electron. Alone and free,
what would he go in search of? A half-remembered
page flashed me an image
of heavenly impregnation: this, I supposed,
he'd rise to when the call came.
But the following day he was back indoors.
All morning, whether pleased

or worried, he travelled the same
light of the bay window as before.

Again I freed him; but yesterday there he was,
crawling like mad, not even trying a new
section of glass. A third time he flicked away
through sunlit air above the flowers.
Siblings? But why so few,
and one at a time, and all but a sixth of the bay
ignored? On the other hand, if this
was an ant apart, a curious male who'd chosen
the mystery of a windowpane
instead of a trumpet-burst of bliss
and a muted dying close,
what have I done?

ACHILL

I

Are you Eagle, the place
where early travellers watched
those great golden birds
hovering over moors?—
or Burned Wood, your homesteads
kindled by raiders' torches
six hundred years ago?
One version grants no more
than hilliness—dark slopes
and crags the drizzle hugs
or a dry wind wipes clean
to do your summits proud.
Be any or all of these—
or even, if you will,
nothing we'd guess. But bear
our dialects, histories, maps:
naming helps us fit
our lives to the wild places.

II

Two of us, your guests
walking in winter, love
the turf-smoke smell, the clinkling
of thicket-covered streams
along the road's edge,
a gorse bush still in bloom,
flat cakes of peat, and the sombre
fells below Slievemore;
opposite, high Minaun
sliced rough to stand in foam,
then waves on a sweep of sand
between white villages—Keel

balancing Dookinella.
More frequently you see us
walking the other way—
ten minutes to Dugort,
where PJ keeps a shop,
Alice her small post office.
Nearby, beneath the crags
and rivulets of Slievemore,
a smooth beach is glazed
by long neat folds of water
gliding from Blacksod Bay.

III

Textures, colours, scents
are yours; the naming ours,
necessary for both
utility and legend.
But sounds and spellings change
when conquerors come: in maps
old meanings lie asleep.
So let me wake, dear Achill
—glossing the names above—
Big Mountain, Fionan's Hill,
Narrows, Cliff-head Sandbank,
Black Field, and once again—
though it seems more than likely
you don't give a puff of wind
for words and images—Eagle.

THE WATERS OF ACHILL

Shades of blue at the northern side,
of green at the southern, the sea round Achill
gave rocky summits drifts of cloud.
Under Slievemore we watched the hail
sweeping towards us in sheer strips
and a moment later were deep in its pelting swarm,
turning away, hearing a torrent of drumtaps
on hooded coats. Quick as it came
the shower was over. Rivulets ran full
in the mountain's bouldered clefts and the bushy
ditches along the road. On a low hill
I plodded dark brown mush
and green squelching sponges, with stick in hand
to test the bog's suck. From those broad slopes
rain oozes down to find
the water table; but here it slips
soapily on my neck and face—
water so soft I'll have to rinse them twice.

KINDLY DECEMBER

I

The warm wind's gusting to force eleven,
booming in the chimney, clawing at trees,
and the electricity's dead. As we peer
through a nervous glow from candle and turf,
something begins to bump in the shrieking
dark outside. I grab a torch,
hunch to the biff of air, and hose
the yard with light. It's the wheelie bin,
down and still being kicked. I heave it
into a corner and pack it firm.

II

Near twelve you say 'The squalls are dying'—and yes,
it's quieter now. From the bedroom window I see
with sudden delight a sky swept for stars,
and the Plough shining clear in the Rainbow's place.
'Nice idea'—I blow the candle out—
'but empty.' Lying beside you then,
slipping towards unconsciousness, I think
'They're never omens. All
natural things, being wonderfully themselves,
are signs of a deeper kind—
instances, evidence, inexhaustible treasuries...'

III

> *Violent storms, with gusts of up to*
> *ninety miles an hour, last night*
> *caused flooding and severe damage*
> *in many parts of the United Kingdom.*

And here? Michael phones the news:
'One of the worst... tiles ripped off...
bushes gone.' A Tyneside friend

writes 'Weather appalling—snowstorms, ice.
You're lucky!' And indeed, with only
things that go bump and sudden blackouts
to cope with, and a cottage huffed
by the Gulf Stream's breath, I think we are.

BORDER CROSSINGS

The first thing I saw one day after getting up
was a sheep with a blue-dyed neck and a red-dyed rump
enjoying a breakfast of leaves from the bush outside
the bedroom window. Three more were having a feed
on a patch of grass when I went for turf. They paused
to size me up, then approached in what I supposed
was a welcoming way as I stood there, pail in hand,
looking back at them in the gentle wind
we shared below the hill. But in fact it was they
who should have been reading welcome signs, not me—
unless, as a sort of grace-and-favour tenant,
I'm under a legal obligation to send
all woolly wanderers packing. 'They cross the river'
I heard, when convinced they couldn't have made it over
or under or through the fence. What 'the river' meant
was a stream in a thicketed gully. I thought 'They *can't*:
the sides are too steep, the bushes are tough and dense'—
but by hell they can, they do, and I've spotted since
the tumble of stones and earth at their crossing point.
Still, unless someone tells me I have to, I won't
be chasing them back. It's true the droppings can be
a nuisance at times, but while I brush them away
I can't help marvelling at the ones that plop
in clusters like kingsize blackberries. As for the sheep
outside the bedroom window, I'm glad it was seen
by me, not a gin-crazed fugitive in a fury
at red-white-and-blue contentedly munching green.

ON THE WIND

'Here you must never say who told you.
Everyone knows what's going on
but they've heard it on the wind.'
I thanked this neighbourly flow of air
(supplier of tales as well as wisdom)
and spoke again of the gospel truths
I'd heard about one event.
But please don't say the wind is fickle:
it's fluent, capacious, Emersonian,
scornful of consistency as
'the hobgoblin of little minds'.
Historical latitude apart,
I can't help wondering if it's true
that *everyone* knows. I heard a voice
swearing 'Poteen? On Achill? No—
that was a long while back.' To which
a second—a drier breeze—replied
'You're joking.' And so began a game
like a reversal of Twenty Questions.
'What do you mean? It's you that's joking.'
'The divil I am. Who is it lives
a mile, maybe, beyond the pub?'
Then architectural hints, followed
by type of vehicle, job, and finally
special interests—poteen aside.
'Jeezez, you don't mean [*tum ti tum*]?'
'I'm telling you nothing.' End of game.
The wind knows also who is or was
sweet on or carrying on with who;
and who, if you're female, you never accept
a lift from, because he'd have his hand
on your leg before he had changed to third.
No less than humans, the wind is keen
on sorrowful stories too: explains
for instance why someone's marriage failed,
or describes a death that happened

for reasons pretty much the same.
Family secrets, private griefs,
turn into whispers, breaths of horror
whiffling in all the lanes and yards.
For news there are sources we can name;
but never forget—at least among
the friendly people of Achill Island—
that gossip, though everywhere, comes from nowhere.

VISITING KEEM
for John F. Deane

'A gem,' you told us. Indeed it was—
and how, walking the southern coast,
could we not think of aquamarine
    and quarried amethyst?
Inseparable that sea, that rock,
sunlight, the sharp wind, and us—
contrasting powers reciprocal
    in one wild loveliness.

Cliffs, islands, luminous green
rumpled and crested by the wind,
long swells becoming glassy scrolls
    that shattered on Dooagh strand,
then far below us, making a writhe
of foam, the clash of rock and wave,
above us crags and ragged streams—
    all these we saw with love.

Sheep with curled horns nibbled grass
on the bank beside the road, where small
cracked telephone poles were tilted quaintly
    or downed by the wind's pull.
We trudged on: all at once, there
was the bay—incomparable, yes,
with headland, soaring hill, buff sand—
    you said we mustn't miss.

Delighted, we looked and looked. But the day
was a short December one, and cloud
was gathering fast with a threat of hail:
    foolish to leave the road
and walk a while on the snug beach
or climb that hill to the fearful rim
where Croaghaun, abruptly ending, drops
    two thousand feet to the foam.

As we travelled back beneath a sky
changed by the play of cloud and sun,
the water lit up randomly
    from Moyteoge to Minaun;
and once, when radiance shafted down
like spotlight beams from heaped grey,
we saw an island rock picked out
    in a pool of silver sea.

Dooagh then, and the flinty hail.
Mary welcomed us, did us proud
not in the bar of her hotel
    but down in the kitchen: bread
and cheese and a pot of tea. She'd gone
to school with the friend we waited for
to drive us home—and yes, had known
    the Deanes for many a year.

THE SETTLEMENT

I

Róisín, serving in the Slievemore Hotel bar,
told us cheerfully how she broke her jaw
when cycling with drink taken but without a lamp,
certain there wasn't a bend where her companion—
lampless too, no doubt—remembered there was;
and Bridget, lonesomely, that her husband died
barely a year ago
of a totally unexpected heart attack.
That, she explained, was why their dog,
who'd been devoted to its master,
had started biting customers' heels.
On the other side of the counter, sitting alone
in the big room almost empty these winter nights,
was John, with specs and a long beard,
who works a knitting machine in Valley.
Back to his house one evening,
he found a couple of windows blasted
by stormy gusts, on the floor a chaos
of glass and wood and rainflood.
We saw, framed at the end of the room,
a photo-view from the side of Krinnuck Hill:
church in the foreground, clear in the middle distance
an L-shape of terraced buildings, hotel included;
Slievemore beyond—one of its finest profiles,
a scalene triangle drawing the fells tight.
One thing was puzzling though: the entire landscape
was empty of trees, yet while we sat there drinking
we heard a grove's branches shredding the wind.
Bridget gave us the simple explanation:
'The photo was taken a hundred years ago:
it's older than the trees.' But she didn't say
the Colony (white letters on sepia ground)
is also called the Settlement. Now we know
that here, close to the cottage we're staying in,
the Achill Mission served provocative soup.

II

The young man travelling the island
in 1831, to meet the peasants,
was Edward Nangle, Church of Ireland minister,
whose official report to the Famine Relief Committee
would detail poverty, squalor, and starvation.
Hence, a few years later, 'the first
Mission Settlement among the native Irish'.
Land from Sir Richard O'Donnell, under
Slievemore's south-eastern face;
dwellings for labourers, scripture readers, teachers;
cultivation of potatoes, oats, and turnips.
Later a church, and from some English friends
a printing press not only for their own language
but also for Irish, Greek and Hebrew.
By 1840 an entire village flourished,
with 'schools, orphanage, hospital, hotel, cornmill,
kiln, grain stores, workshops, hardware shop,
stables, and many cottages'—
                      Stop!
How did the islanders feel about
this takeover bid, this imperialistic package?
Well, some of them joined—and the gift of food
for wasted bodies helped no end in the work
of changing Catholic souls to Protestant ones.
Those 'Jumpers', otherwise 'Soupers', alarmed the faithful,
many of whom assaulted the mission folk,
while Nangle used the printing press like a gun
for counter-attacks of argument and invective
against his clerical foes. The war grew hotter
when Catholic schools were founded to undermine
the undermining doctrines of the invader.
Well-meaners all, the righteous versus the righteous,
the dedicated damning the dedicated;
human hearts, after millennia, still
savaging human hearts. But the local storm
dies out and the air starts blustering somewhere else:
all that's left of the work of Edward Nangle

is the ministry of a little church
between Slievemore and Krinnuck.

III

St. Thomas's: arched ceiling
with beams as dark as turf; walls pale pink;
brightly coloured windows beyond the altar.
Today we shared the pew of a friendly neighbour
who hoped we'd attend the carol service
'to swell the congregation'.
Someone up at the front put records on
—a rich-toned choir, a noble-hearted organ—
and twenty modest carollers sang along
in peaceful adoration. How demanding
those sweet perpetual melodies and verses,
at least for some who love them: even playing
the tunes alone at times, I feel
uneasy—both the delighted child
and the unbelieving adult. Faithful few,
pardon me for taking the starry scenes
as true in a mythic way—as variations
on themes perennial and universal
secreted in human history.
Even the words outside
St. Thomas's put the heart first—
loving before believing:
Welcome friend and stranger...
Our outlook is truly ecumenical...
'Looking out' on the gentle slopes between
church and hotel, I feel that something
the mission never dreamed of has been achieved
since the ladle dipped for the last time,
and hope that people a thousand years from now,
understanding what they all have in common,
and what they share deep down
with fox and heron, trees, moorland, mountain,
the sea, the wind, the stars,
will sometimes pray without a word.

IN THE BUS SHELTER

After a goodnight kiss he waits
at the stop still called The School.
Beyond a crust of wall demanding
TERMINATE TORY SCUM,
a void above scorched rubble
lets him see terrace chimneys,
the glow of drawn curtains.
Floodlit in front of splashing tyres
the rain sparks like static.
He shivers, peers through wind
where clobbered glass cascaded;
thinks of firelight, conversation,
the music and love he makes
with one her pupils loved as well,
and someone's hurt becoming
a mob of flames high on petrol.

THE CIRCLING BEAM

Land and ocean
break each other; are fickle
with boats—the wave
fondling or battering, rock
a haven or troubled grave.

The boats are neutral,
risking the fractious border,
carrying fish and people
past headland foam
to the wharf below the chapel.

Prayers, codes, lamps.
On waves around the island
a sweep of silver; here
a star's even pulse
through night and fear.

EPITHALAMION (1992)
for Peter and Sue

Some people face the table, some the altar;
I'm in-betweenish!—thinning out the Bible's
authority through filter after filter,
but still enchanted by the pipes and bells.

Let changes then be rung for Peter, Susan,
Alizon, Dominic, Rose, Molly, Sam;
and for deep universals—love and reason,
justice, honesty, courage, work, dream.

Let personal and abstract weave one river
of humnotes and harmonics: joyful waves—
though choice contend with chance and now with never—
declare the consonance of seven lives.

Dear newlyweds, let soundflow become wind
to make you warmth and light, to bring you many
colours of sky and earth, to be a hand
stroking the moor below the Hills o' Wanny.

ATTRACTIONS

Even more than toffee apples,
the dodgems' dithery dunting,
or music pumped for riders
bobbing in slow motion,
I loved the taut thread
from brain to target, the soft
pull that made an airgun
sneeze and butt my neck,
the thrill of putting another dot
inside a nest of rings.

Words are as far from pellets
as Primum Mobile was from Earth,
but some things are equally prized
by poets, geometers,
boys in the firing booth.

TO JON SILKIN (1930-1997)

Jon, you were one of a few I found
so different as to be frightening—
not in their manner, but in the demands
they made on themselves and the world.
You were good to me: I'm grateful,
also slightly ashamed to have kept
a wary distance, but we are what we are.
I think of lives that flourish
in scalding springs, close
to the ocean's troubled bed,
and all the others from middle range
to upper—dolphins playing
in translucent fathoms, flying fish
skimming the sunny surface.
Crude perhaps, but you know how hard it is
to find a perfect metaphor. This one says
diverse, not deep or shallow—includes even
the whale and the bathysphere! Still,
your poems are often deep, quite near
the faulted rock and the lava,
exacting. But no more of that.
Thanks again for the times we ate together,
the times you honoured reluctant me
with strong-willed argument, and the times
you made me like my verse.
Forgive me that through the years,
strong-willed in a different way,
I guarded my own space, fearing
disturbance from your richer gift,
your drives and your convictions.
Recently, though you'd had a bad night,
you were just as keen and friendly—
your heart mending, you said.
And I said, after we'd talked a while
in the ward, after you'd strolled with me
along the corridor and we'd gripped hands,
'See you next week'. I still see
your warm courageous smile.

THE LANGUAGE MAN

'Partridge is in a pear-tree of his own'
(Howard on *Origins*). Yes, and hopped alone
year after year, his labour also fun,
in branches growing so far towards the sun
it must have seemed at times they'd never end.
Honour and thank him, poets, as your friend.

POETRY GIGS, 1994

New rock 'n' roll? Without iambics? Please,
we're listening but a bit confused. How come
you cavil at the beat of lines like these
yet love the insistent metre of a drum?

BIOGRAPHIES (1959)

Finally anger freed him. Year by year
his elders lost their scruples, he his fear,
and facing frank rejection he could learn
to light the fuse of truth and let it burn.
His parting insult banged like gelignite
on walls of crass conformity and spite.

Another version tells of 'love' oozing
from pinched minds; no crisis and no choosing,
but a long ache of bafflement, of tedium.
Explosives couldn't beat that sticky medium:
hurt, afraid of hurting, he slouched away—
puppet on strings of glue till his dying day.

THE SONG OF THE CROSSWORD PUZZLER (1990)
for Kate because she likes crosswords

My love, you're like a zinfandel,
   Piquante and mydriatic—
Yet sometimes more like hydromel,
   So simple, so villatic.
       Your lips are red as ladybirds,
       Your eyes effulge, and oh! your words
Upwaft me in a wild chandelle,
   Even when they are phatic.

Thank heaven I'm a thermophile
   Since you're so pyrogenic:
My heart's now strongly pulsatile
   Where once it was asthenic.
       As Gaia makes the earth rotate,
       Your fires produce, to activate
This jubilant eolipile,
   A power that's doubly phrenic.

You're dolphin, I am tubifex,
   You're musky, I'm thionic;
I'm zero where you're googolplex,
   At odds where you're syntonic.
       But though some choice hyperbole
       Enriches every line you see,
I swear, my houri and my hex,
   I've never been gnathonic.

PART TWO

TO WILLIAM CARLOS WILLIAMS

Only in things? Drawn by book and window,
all morning I've been loving
flowers, trees, clouds,
but also, like the shining air they move in,
a flood of abstract thought.

Beliefs aside, a limpid argument
can have the immediacy of wind
flowing among the leaves,
or be for mind what clear water gliding
on stones can be for eye and dipping hand.

How easily one man's preference
turns to a cult, advice thickens to dogma,
talent conforms. Although we cherish you,
maybe the time has come for reason
to float away your idea about ideas.

FROM A PARSON'S JOURNAL

Studying long and hard, I mastered all
we were taught about the truths and heresies.
The Trinity, the Creation and the Fall,
the Virgin Birth, the Resurrection: these
were well-tried waters, channels of the divine—
entirely safe, I thought, for ships like mine.

In those days, who could have guessed a jagged reef
would rip my faith? At times I can only pray
'Lord, I believe; help Thou mine unbelief'—
a poor weapon to keep despair at bay,
but all I have. Smiling my clerical smile
I wonder if folk detect a hint of guile.

Am I being tested? Perhaps. At all events
it can't be good to ignore the new. I read
assiduously the latest arguments
and often find them telling: it's then I need
a brain stronger than mine to affirm the old,
persuade me nothing can break the credal mould.

What *is* believing? That's where I'm all at sea.
Some say one thing, some another; but most
conceive as factual, so it seems to me,
our Father 'up' in heaven, the Holy Ghost,
Adam's orchard, the maiden mother, and Christ,
a man-god, rising after being sacrificed:

as I conceived them, and my teachers too,
but having it both ways, seeing unlikely things
as symbols or mysteries. What can I hold as *true*
when fear of failure comes with its evil wings?
In the pulpit now I feel that I'm in the dock!
God bless my pastoral visits, my trusting flock.

AZTEC PICTURE

The rider carrying shield and cross
has raised his heavy sword to slash
a native bearing a gift of fruit.

The soldier standing below the steps,
from which a comrade smiles and waves,
has sliced a body into pieces.

What kind of god, some ask, desires
blood so pitiful, spilled without
the altar and the priest's knife.

AFTER THE BRIEFING

Dear Father, bless our mission:
help us to kill
numerous others of
your daughters and your sons,
our sisters and our brothers.
And thanks, oh Lord,
that now, to do your will,
you grant us, not the sword,
but nuclear fission.

ELECTRICITY

    She screamed in hell each time
he let the monster out, kept saying no
    each time he caged it; found a flow
of will and voice human enough to cry
'Aren't you a person also, just like me,
with friends and mate and children? Don't you *see*?'

    Grew weaker—body worn,
personality fading; but a light
    still shone from deepening caves, her right
still challenged his. In Medical Wing her heart
was rested so that he, with every spurt
of power, could still dislodge a little dirt.

    His parents had been strict,
loyal to Church and Commerce and the State.
    He cherished words like *pure* and *great*,
worried about his lapses. Neither fool
nor high flyer, too middling to rebel,
he opted for interrogating well.

    Spent years being firm, clear,
unsentimental for his country's sake
    (and God's of course). Now comes awake
in the coronary unit, where a nurse
and a sister watch intently, and the juice
he meted pain with has a different use.

THE WAYS OF PROVIDENCE

A black in Denver city;
two whites, each with a gun.

When a white woman cried
'Please stop! Leave him alone!',

they shot the black, then her:
a bullet smashed her spine.

For being so brave and loving
she'll never walk again.

As wife, husband, children
bear unexpected pain—

all five each other's added
sickeningly to their own—

and share the steely thought
'Was it right to intervene?',

their faith in God the Father
is tested to the bone.

SONGS OF PRAISE

Don't glorify the works of God
unless you can include them all—

as well as soul and star and clod
(Browning), and flower in crannied wall
(Tennyson), the longing of men's parts
to flower in the crannied flesh;
volcanoes, pythons, pimples, farts,
grim futures hatching in the creche—

because a universal law
will cancel any line you draw.

WHAT COMES NATURALLY

Ours lasts a moment, yours
through all the violent years
from Bang to Crunch. We're told you suffer:
you are the stung caterpillar,
motionless but undead,
as well as the fattening grub inside;
lion and zebra, both
feeling the huge teeth
bloodily fasten; parents and two-year-old
bound in torment, she in a weird nonworld
from birth, wretchedly dying,
and they longing, praying
(you praying in vain to you)
that either you let her go
tomorrow or make her well.
No: how could you will
your own anguish, how be the teeming One
but rapturously? We have this token,
the charged seconds, a small
shock of ecstasy; you the whole
of spacetime, a prodigal self-delighting fall.

THE IDEALIST

How could the same self
migrate from man to man,
let alone man to wolf?
And why should a Will beyond
both good and evil plan
deliverance through a round
of many lives, or even
care that the human mind
broods over guilt and sin?

I think we have only one
arrival, and what we need
release from isn't sin:
it's ego-bound illusion
splitting a world that's really
a whole diversified.
But seeing whole depends on
being whole, or holy—
on having light within.

How can we make the dark
falter, the flame begin,
unless by thinking whole—
of kinship, the all-in-one,
rain as a spectral arc.
Soul cherishing soul
is the blindness known as sin
being turned to vision: work
the saints are expert in.

UNDER THE RAINBOW

Sophie has gone—abducted and raped, then murdered.
Seven years old. All who are not indifferent
try to imagine, then not imagine, what Sophie
went through, and what her parents are going through,
and what they'll have to endure as long as they live.
Wallace, thank God, is safely behind bars.

But if we think of him burying his face in his hands
when the judge described him, and spending the rest of his life
in the grip of memory, like a wolf in a trap,
or pondering a chaplain's words as, drop by drop,
seconds make icy years, and dying at last
in the hope that he's earned forgiveness, how do we feel?

And how, if we think of horrors the whole way through
from earthquakes to ethnic cleansing—think perhaps
of creatures becoming food (some swallowed alive),
flare-ups in families, crimes of passionate pride,
muggings and maimings, batons battering blacks,
obsessions, impulses, craziness taking over,

of ideological fallout spreading wide,
and weapons made out of words, which we've all wielded—
some used as well as the sticks and stones, while others
have hurt by themselves but sometimes far more deeply,
in home and playground, palace and parliament,
in offices, workshops, courtrooms, even in church:

how, my dear, can we hope that the dream of wholeness
—of seeing and being whole, of a healed world—
can ever be more than a dream? I try to believe,
I listen and try to believe, but again and again
my thought of the blood and the broken hearts and the broken
lives sweeps in like a flashflood over fields.

EVOLUTION

... intensely hot, and arid apart from a
flashflood once in a while.
I ride here as frequently as I can
to be alone with the hard clean stillness—
great bluffs rising from dust and boulders into
naked blue, their vast
crumple of sun and shadow.

Maybe you'll think I'm mad,
but more and more I have the feeling
the world should have stayed like this.
Please don't misunderstand: I admire,
if sometimes in a shivery way,
the needled plants and the spiders and diamondbacks;
even scorpions are little marvels.
But having to live was how the dying began.

From a letter in *Christian Update*: 'What about
the anthropic principle?' Well,
what about it? Humans are here because
the universe evolved in a special way,
but did it evolve like that
so humans could be here? I have a friend
who firmly believes it did, but where's the proof?

This common sky was witness to rival prayers,
bows answering guns, charred corpses,
and greed growing genocidal.
True, there was violence even without life—
still is, from quark to quake.
The bluff's primordial grain is broken down
by wind and sudden water.
But rocks have no cells, no appetites, no distress,
and that's one reason I turn to them for healing.

It's strange: when I'm near the mesa,
some part of me becomes
crystalline, very sure and calm, as though
enfolded by a forebear who never died.
I like to think of this as a step towards
nibbana, the coolness (they say) of being
free from self in a deep dark radiance.

Too much, too much! Sorry! I'll write
more newsily the next time. Love to you all.

LAZINESS

What is it? Certainly not the same
 as idleness; rather, a longing to be idle.
But that's like saying 'lame'
 and leaving out the reason. Dull, Dull,
Dull the heartbell tolls, chime after doleful chime:
 death-wish, is that what it is?
Many then from an early age
 have forced themselves to live, or been forced by others,
day after day heaving a new page
 up and over like an iron lid.
No one's surprised where damage
 was circumstantial—parents dead
or divorced when most needed, or struggling on in hate,
 maybe in want: where any bad luck has caused
a child's will to degenerate,
 imagination to see a door closed
that once was open to light.
 For some, misfortune arrived
later: there are grey-haired women we know
 as smilers getting along, who, bereaved
or in bodily pain or fearing death, show
 the world what it wants to see, saying to themselves
'Millions suffer far more than you';
 but for whom, out of our sight, each day dissolves
in a dismal pool of inertia, of putting off,
 in desire for sleep, even the sleep they fear.
A voice silently cries, though forbidden, 'I've had enough!
 Please let me rest! I worked, I tried to care;
year after year I took the rough
 uncomplainingly with the smooth'—and we'd assent if we heard,
being human and humane.
 But how about younger people reared
in comfort, who attain
 what they and their loving parents hoped, or more,
yet feel that all they do is against the grain
 except (including!) the sensual thrills, the poor

lazy escapes from laziness? Ask the saints
    and the Bhodisattvas. Nothing can make you free,
Gautama said, but mind undoing the constraints
    of partiality, dispossessing the 'I'
that continually invents
    itself and a world to act in, no more real
than dreams recalled on waking. Do those lives
    of far-from-idle laziness, of denial
within acceptance, of uncommitted drives,
    secrete a lonely awareness it's hard to understand—
some sense of a truth below what the plausible self believes,
    waiting like hidden water to be divined?
No death-wish there, but an inward search for release
    from wrong perception, troublesome appetites,
a heart rarely at peace:
    for the radiance that illuminates
without casting shadows—free of space,
    free of time, yet here and now we're told—
light enough for the whole human race
    if only our minds could break the selfish mould.

FEMINA: A RHAPSODY

I am the whore and the holy one,
I am the wife and the virgin...
—'Thunder, Perfect Mind', a Gnostic poem

Dark from the darker Void,
Mother of All, forever one
with the Father of All, how you have
haunted us through the wrangling ages!
Yin, Shakti, Sophia, Holy Spirit,
Anima Mundi; Lilith before you were Eve,
escaping from Adam's arrogance to become
night-flyer, screech-owl, demon.
A soapstone doll with buttocks
trying to sprout wings!
Great Isis, your brother's wife,
mother of Horus and his Pharaohs.
Terrifying Kali; Ishtar, goddess of war
as well as love and abounding earth;
Ceres with golden sheaves; pure Artemis
with arrows of silver moonlight,
hunter-protector of woodland beasts,
protector of hunted virgins; Aphrodite
rising naked from the Cyprian foam;
priestess and harlot of the temple;
La Belle Dame Sans Merci; and lately—
strong though denatured after Peter and Paul,
strong in the oily wake of progress—
Mae, Marlene, Marilyn; page three girl,
vamp of the centre spread, a chatline voice,
a thrill on some dreamy website. Mother of All,
your moon fades in the dawn of science,
but still you are strong: now you are fire bursting
from quantum foam and spreading
with unbelievable power to compose the stars!
We adore you still, still you are drawing us in
as wife, lover, whore—partly because
your light comes from your darkness, and your darkness
comes from the deeper darkness of the Void.

NOCTURNE

Lovely
   lovely the deep
      of stars

the stillness
   of lake and hill
      in dark light

and then the quick
   of here as a
      fish glints.

O Black Madonna,
   bride of Christ, I
      thee worship also.

AT THE MOONLIT POOL: A PASTORAL

'Thank heaven the mind I see you with
transforms reality to myth,
calming a three-horned beast whose pain
is hellfire. May your flesh remain
this magic of the silversmith.'

'Thank *you*, my lord, for being so nice,
for sparing me the scorch of vice;
but why, I wonder, do you need
myths to avoid a cruel deed?
Must I be pure at such a price?'

'Forgive me, lady, but a man
of honour does the best he can.
You see me gladly goddess-charmed
so neither you nor I be harmed
by what the brutal blood began.'

'My lord, I think I understand.
Perhaps, if you would take my hand,
you'd find it flesh again, my trust
an opening flower, and your lust
no longer sighing in wonderland.'

THE UTOPIAN

The feminists are right.
No wonder women, trapped for so many years,
are hammering on the bars.

The masculists are right.
No wonder, given the power of womanhood,
husbands have been so bad.

Blame nature, evolution,
God if you will: there's no way man and wife
can avoid the common grief

unless by the way of love
so unpossessive they loose the sexual tie,
making each other free

while still the best of friends
and still loving their children. Women, men,
surely it can be done!

THEOLOGIES

If there's anyone up there
it's only fair
he should be partly she,
don't you agree?

As for that cryptic stuff
—Brahman, the Void, Ein Sof—
well, I prefer
a darkness I can see.

A PROFESSOR TO SOME FRIENDS

I

So here you have God and nothingness, *nothingness*, then
(a misleadingly temporal word, but we can't avoid it)
a huge explosion, a violent ejaculation—
orgasmic, let us suppose!—of time and space
and radiant energy, initiating a world
that will go on expanding for billions and billions of years.
Energy? Well, the scientist's definition
is 'capacity to do work'. That's pretty abstract;
but E, you remember, equals *mc squared*,
which is a way of saying, to put it simply,
that mass is condensed energy. Now, if you mix
the abstract with the concrete, what do you get?
The energy that exploded out of nothing
was fiery and finite: so here, I propose, is God
starting a measure of material work.
Is God the worker? Maybe, maybe not.
Either way it's obvious that he's mad.
Of course there's *order*, there's lots and lots of order—
that's what we mean by cosmos; but those who think
there's a plan behind it all, or might be a plan,
should remember 'method in madness'—the logic, say,
of paranoiacs. However: worker or not,
designer or not, this God we're postulating
started a process. We call it evolution.

II

Fundamental particles to begin with,
trillions on trillions dancing their random dance,
as poetic scientists say. Have you ever seen
a dance that resembled chaos, a dance like the flitting
of midges?—though these are vast and extremely slow
compared with quanta, and they never collide.
But let's forget about chaos: more fundamental

than fundamental particles are the laws
that make a process possible, represented
by neat equations and corresponding words.
To cut a long story short, collisions at last
resulted in coalescence. Neutrons and protons,
bound by the strongest of four forces, became
the nuclear part of ions: hence the plasmic
blaze of galaxies. These, like silver dots
on a black balloon being blown bigger and bigger,
are moving farther apart. But that's not all:
competing for space, some galaxies swallow others.
Our own, just one among many billions, contains
a few hundred billion stars where others can boast
thousands of billions. Now, consider our sun,
no more than an average star in the Milky Way;
behold our earth, one of its minor planets,
and then what we derive from—organic acids,
chancy progenitors of DNA, concocted
in muddy pools with the help of sun and lightning.

III

Much later there were amoebas, unicellular
swimming blobs—and here again you perceive
the divine madness. But let me pause for a moment
to recapitulate. Out of the timeless void
sprang energy, out of that a prodigious swarm
of colliding particles; then the nucleons joined
and captured electrons; ionised atoms composed
the stars, in which (let me add) were generated
the heavier elements.—Well, on our speck of rock
it was much the same. The mechanism of life,
being God's invention, could only start all over
with smallness and then proceed to bigness: hence
the violent evolution from single cells
to multicellular units. Even amoebas,
minute, slimy, amorphous, enrich themselves
in galactic style—one gorging on another

as well as on tinier things—until they're ready
to reproduce by fission. You see how it goes:
first an expanding universe, then a part
that becomes an expanding biosphere. Each damn species
branches out of an earlier by a means
worse than a lottery—glitches in the helix
causing innovations lucky enough
to help in the crazy adaptive competition
while others must come to nothing. And so you have
this weird mélange, from micro to macroscopic.
Protozoa go busily on and on;
heavyweights, grand survivors in their day,
prove vulnerable—the dinosaurs wiped out
by natural forces, whales and elephants threatened
by human greed and its merciless instruments.

IV

Ah, humans, humans! This is where priests and prophets,
and some professors and poets, flap their wings
and soar towards the sublime. 'Of course,' they cry,
'ants and ermines perpetuate their kind
for the sake of perpetuation' (or, in the words
of some sentimental hymns, to praise their Maker);
'but don't forget evolution, the drive toward
perfection, ending in Man' (never in Woman),
'who as yet is far from perfect, but who has achieved
such wonderful works—empires, philosophies, scriptures,
statues and palaces, epics and operas, sciences
endlessly probing; and think of the pioneers
who made advances possible—brain or brawn,
or both, engaging the powers of spirit and will
to the glory of Homo Sapiens'—or of God.
Well, we're all entitled to our opinion.
Mine, as I've said (and of course I apologise
to any I may have hurt), is that God—supposing
he even exists, which I very much doubt—is mad;
but if he does, and if we're made in his image,
clearly our lack of sapience boosts my claim.

V

Let me offer you two undeniable facts:
first, evolution; second, perennial pain.
Both imply conflict, the second those modes of conflict
intrinsic to life. We know perennial pain
as humans, and we assume it for chimpanzees,
for horses and dogs and cats, and then (why not?)
for millions of species we haven't domesticated—
pain for the predator sometimes, always pain
for the captured prey. And where should we draw the line?
Lizards? Crabs? Be that as it may, we observe
a destined spiral of life gorging on life
and getting nowhere—at least below the summit
of evolution. The wasps and the worms go on
being nothing but wasps and worms; on the other hand
you have men becoming gods (our presidents, popes,
pop stars, crooks, tycoons), but the masses too,
their longings just as intense, who find themselves
going round and round, each generation begetting
another *ad infinitum*. For what, I ask you?
Shakespeare? Mozart? Newton? Hegel and Marx?
Is a symphony worth millennia of painful conflict,
of poverty, hunger, disease, exhausting labour?
'But what about Progress?' *Hah!* Pictures from space,
rapacious banks and multinationals; meanwhile
trees and people massacred, filthy air
and filthy water, global warming, a hole
in the ozone layer. You see what the fireball started,
what evolution produced; and if both derived
from the mind of God—if God exists—the only
sane conclusion is that he's mad, mad, mad.

FIRST PERSON

'You're not the only pebble on the beach'
my elders used to say—
wisely, although conflating *I* with *each*
ignored the grey of *most*.
                        The Indian way
thins *I* to a kind of ghost
bodied life after life till the plenum-void
slips it from maya's mesh.
                            What toiled from clay
to brainy anthropoid
now prefers microchips to DNA,
metal to bone and flesh.
Its cruel agents are dreaming of a day
when robots croaking 'I'
will mean it, circuited then to love and grieve,
be furious, frightened, bored.
                                   Should sapiens die,
the self that he adored
as hero, angel, god-king may survive,
those androids labour on
in endless pain, their sensitive silicon
obedient to the Ray.

FOR THE MILLENNIUM PRAYERBOOK

Lord, let not
my ego swell
and blaze like a supernova
while my collapsing soul
becomes its own hell,
a black hole
that will swallow
even a friend drawn
closer in troubled orbit,
and be all alone
unless connected by
a wormhole
to a soul as lost and hollow.

RECYCLING
> *Did you know that every time you take a breath you inhale about a hundred atoms that were once in Julius Caesar?*
> —BBC Learning Zone

No I didn't, but it seems to follow
from what I did—that we are all composed
of stardust, we are all
billions of years old. I would have chosen
Gautama, say, or Kant, but the point is
I'm breathing everybody who's dead and gone,
and possibly you as well.

Still there are people so obsessed with blood
they resemble Hitler: fools, dangerous fools.
Like it or not, we're all
atomically united. I'll think of that
the next time one whose nerves no doubt I get on
gets on my nerves and makes me want to kill.

KEEPING UP

Quantum foam and baby universes!
Natural selection in superspace! What next?
We're out of touch, it seems, if we even ask
how the laws began that could evolve a star
from a burst of radiation. They simply *are*:

as the super-ocean of energy just *is*—
mysterious as 'God', 'Nature', the 'Void',
and equally awesome. So, while astrophysics
boils with theology in an acrid brew,
the mystic calmly flavours old with new.

HEISENBERG IN COPENHAGEN

'Not nature in itself, but nature
exposed to our method of questioning.'
Did that disturb you, or were you glad
some truth would outreach for ever
the equations and the measuring rod?
I'd like to have been there, that blue midnight,
when you strolled on the promenade
with Pauli, and spoke of the soul and Pascal's 'fire'—
mysteries presupposed
by the lovely patterns they elude—
and a liner gliding past, 'its bright lights
fabulous and unreal', made
you think about intentions, formative power,
a consciousness you couldn't quite call God.

THE SEEKER

Then alone do we know God truly, when we believe that He is far above all that man can possibly conceive of God.
—Thomas Aquinas

When it comes to atoms, language can be used only as in poetry.
—Niels Bohr

I

Mystical, misty! That's what people think,
    and often as not they link
'mystic' with 'magic' and 'paranormal' and all
    the dottier New Age stuff, a sprawl
of daydream and pseudo-science. But real science,
    believe me, makes good sense,
not least in its patient unexpected growth
    toward mysticism: from both
we learn the strange lesson that rock and steel
    are insubstantial though they feel
so hard at our fingertips. Should we complain
    if new equations go with the grain
of old beliefs, if even physicists find
    the world an effect of mind?
A tangible void is what the sages teach
    in their metaphor-mining speech:
the richness we call reality is appearance,
    maya, lila, Shiva's dance,
or (from another country) the Tao at play.
    But Void is only a way
of saying transcendent, naming what can't be thought
    by philosophers, or be caught
in the nets of popular faith. Such a gathering in
    of notions about original sin,
karma, reincarnation, heaven and hell!
    'Thy word is all, if we could spell'
sang Herbert, one of the priests who understood
    more than their fellows could.

II

But please don't think me aloof or inhumane.
    Day after day the pain
of the earth's millions makes my heart protest—
    my mind also: how can I rest,
pulled one way by the voice of love and justice,
    another by knowing that this
outrageous world may be as it has to be?
    We fret about 'you' and 'me'—
how could we not?—but human beings are one
    with the biosphere, the sun,
the galaxies, then the clouds of gas and dust,
    and the nucleons after the first
few moments of nature's rule, as space and time
    went flooding out: all these a sublime
prolific sequence, but violent through and through.
    There could have been nothing new
in the heavens, or here on land or in the ocean,
    unless there'd been integration;
but conflict's the other side of that: there'd be
    no gases, no stars to see,
if particles hadn't collided, often annihilating
    each other, till a kind of mating
produced the atoms. And there you've a paradigm
    of life: for cellular slime,
for reptile and ape and human, for gut and brain,
    primordial laws obtain.
The need to have space, to join, to eat, can still
    make Anthropos court and kill.

III

Why are we saddened now by hate and war?
    Does the feeling that makes us more
than familial, tribal, nationalist, derive
    from the integrative drive
that earlier made us those? My answer's yes,

though it's only a hopeful guess.
Granted that the cosmos is One and Many,
   both of these words imply
integrity: each of the Many is also one.
   But every thread of the All is spun
from the same immaterial stuff: a tangible 'thing',
   though unique, has no separate being.
Nor has a family, a tribe, a nation—each
   the self extending its reach.
And yet, though we plead the Species, and therefore Earth,
   are surely of greater worth
(in what might be called the ecumenical sense),
   still the planet is tense
with enmities old or new, and in many places—
   homelands of rival races
or sects or factions—is bloodied by open warfare
   or sneaky bombs. The despair
of innocents—orphaned children, women as wives,
   as mothers, bereaved by knives,
grenades, bullets—haunts, year after year,
   the screen where the ads appear.

IV

The Void, being far beyond anything we conceive,
   is beyond both good and evil.
Wholeness, the One's integrity: out of this
   (if you'll grant a hypothesis)
comes moral concern—its root compassion, its bole
   the sense of justice. The 'soul
of the world', or Pascal's 'fire', has filled the hearts
   of only a few, but we're all parts
of the One, and people who know or feel they are
   cherish others as far
as the world's ways allow—repulse or kill
   only against their will,
taking the life of plant or beast to live,
   being forced perhaps to give

blow for blow defending the weak when thugs
    high on power or drugs
break in to shatter homes. Perennial hate,
    perennial love: by the laws of nature
that's what the world is like. So I listen still
    to the few who wait until
the enchantment comes, who say that within the strife
    there's another kind of life,
beyond all understanding, all common feeling,
    profound and calm and healing.

TO THE LADY OF NORWICH

Dear Julian, I've been reading you again,
and now—forgive me—can't restrain my pen!
I love your mind, so gentle and so strong,
so clear too, and the little stream of song
within your reasoned prose—though, sad to say,
'All manner of thing shall be well' becomes today
'Everything is going to be all right'. I think
you'd say 'All right! Surely the mental link
matters more than the words'—and I'd agree
while my love of song protested. You and me,
and others like me, still communicating
after six hundred years—though some keep waiting
where you received assurance—is the fact
that makes me write this letter, a sort of pact!
You loved courtesy: let me now try,
courteously, to say what you and I—
people like me—might share two years before
the will of God (your teaching) swings the door
to another century.
                    Many now say Chance,
others the Void. For some it's Shiva's dance
that shapes the world—a myth you'd hardly know,
implying that what seems real isn't so:
yet this—how did the questioning begin?—
is your account of evil (you call it 'sin').
You died in the tight embrace of Mother Church
before the western mind renewed a search
that began in Ancient Greece. We've moved as far
from what you were—what in your book you *are*—
as others, several centuries from now,
will have moved from us—the simpler wondering how
we could have believed such nonsense.
                                  Chance or Cause?
(I leave out 'caused by chance'!) Our natural laws
admit the random (puzzlingly), but for you
everything's willed by God. If that is true,

how can you match your tenderest belief—
that 'our Father' is wholly loving—with the grief
of sinners he willed to sin: above all, those
millions of sons and daughters he never chose
for heaven, or, in other words, chose for hell?
Also (sorry!) the notion that 'Adam' fell
and the works of 'the Fiend and his set' explain our ills
is false for most of us now, when modern skills
challenge the ones you trusted.—*Pax, pax!*
Had I been living when priest and crucifix
were so important, it's likely that I too
would have considered all the dogmas true.

   I wonder what you'd think if you'd been born
in this wild century: whether you'd be torn,
as many are, between the old and new,
or whether you'd be one of those—the few?—
who feel there's no division. Some of us,
half bored and half attracted by the fuss
of science versus religion, see no quarrel
between the scientific and the moral,
at heart the mystical. Would you understand,
if you were living now, that there's a strand
running through all religions—spirit, soul,
whatever—that informs us of the Whole
we all belong to? I suspect you would.
Christian sanctity, Bodhisattvahood—
is there any difference? Only in the style,
the creed, the legend: you for a little while
saw tortured Christ, others some Eastern face—
more likely nothing. I hope you'd say that grace
is universal, no one could be denied
the supreme love: Christian and 'pagan' pride
should burn in cleansing flames, pre-heavenly fire,
not in eternal hell. Was your desire
for private pain, fused with your hope of bliss,
so selfless?

          Forgive me. I'll add no more than this:
Of all your revelations, the ones I most

respond to are the seventh and twelfth: first
your sense, utterly peaceful, of an abounding
love; then knowledge, too deep for understanding,
of the unique Self. 'I who am all'
is the greatest of binding-songs, of words that call
quietly through the ages: words that spell
your homelier truth, 'All manner of thing shall be well'.

NOTES

Energies (p. 33)
In modern cosmology the phrase 'finite and unbounded' is applied hypothetically to the whole of space, which is regarded as spherical and therefore as having no natural *linear* limits. 'Black and white' is suggestive partly of yin and yang. The simple device is a radiometer, whose globe-enclosed 'whirligig' is activated by the energy of sunlight.

Epithalamion (p. 53)
Lines 13-14: at the time of writing, the poet Peter Bennet used windpower to generate electricity for his cottage in Northumberland.

Attractions (p. 54)
The target's nested rings are like a chart depicting the concentric spheres of Ptolemaic cosmology. The largest sphere was the Primum Mobile. The short list in the last two lines could be greatly extended, starting with people who like the precision of darts, archery and football!

The Song of the Crossword Puzzler (p. 59)
Zinfandel: a dry Californian wine. *Mydriatic*: causing dilation of the eye pupils. *Hydromel*: water and honey. *Villatic*: rustic. *Chandelle*: in aviation, an abrupt soaring turn. *Phatic*: trivially sociable. *Thermophile*: a heat-loving creature. *Pyrogenic*: heat-producing. *Asthenic*: feeble. *Eolipile*: a hollow ball mounted over flames and rotated by steam. *Phrenic*: of the mind and the diaphragm. *Tubifex*: a small worm, known as sewage or river worm. *Thionic*: sulphurous. *Googolplex*: 1 plus a googol of zeros. Googol: 1 plus 100 zeros. *Syntonic*: in tune with one's environment. *Hex*: a witch. *Gnathonic*: sycophantic.

To William Carlos Williams (p. 63)
'No ideas but in things'—William Carlos Williams

For the Millennium Prayerbook (p. 87)
I'd like 'ego' to be pronounced with a long *e*! In astrophysics, a wormhole is 'a cosmic subway connecting two black holes' (John Gribbin's definition in his *Companion to the Cosmos*).